THE CIVIL RIGHTS ERA

History SparkNotes

SPARKNOTES is a registered trademark of SparkNotes LLC

Spark Publishing
A Division of Barnes & Noble Publishing
120 Fifth Avenue
New York, NY 10011
www.sparknotes.com

ISBN-13: 978-1-4114-0421-2
ISBN-10: 1-4114-0421-1

Library of Congress information available upon request.

Please submit changes or report errors to www.sparknotes.com/errors.

Printed and bound in the United States.

1 3 5 7 9 10 8 6 4 2

CONTENTS

OVERVIEW

Many history textbooks characterize the civil rights era as a discrete event that happened between the 1950s and 1970s, casting only a brief glance at its historical context. But this mid-twentieth-century struggle for racial equality that we call the modern civil rights movement was actually the pinnacle of a struggle that had begun nearly a century earlier, during the Reconstruction era of the late 1860s and 1870s.

After the Civil War, Congress passed a series of civil rights laws, and the states ratified three amendments to the Constitution to protect former slaves. A combination of economic depression and underhanded tactics by southern politicians, however, prevented former slaves from taking advantage of these freedoms. As a result, many southern blacks returned to virtual economic bondage as sharecroppers working for white landowners, while "black codes" kept them in a position of social inferiority. As a result, nearly a century after emancipation, blacks still sat at different tables than whites, used different bathrooms, made far less money, and had little chance for universal integration.

Events in the 1940s and 1950s prompted some blacks to push harder for equality than their predecessors. Segregationist policies in the South and the need for more skilled workers in the North had driven many blacks to move to northern cities in the period between World War I and World War II. This massive movement of blacks from the South to the North became known as the Great Migration. Urbanized blacks also benefited greatly from the postwar economic boom during the 1950s and received additional support from unions and the Democratic Party. One NAACP leader noted that these newfound experiences awakened many black Americans to the extreme injustice of segregation.

After World War II, civil rights leaders capitalized on America's struggle for freedom and democracy abroad during the Cold War. Even though more than a million blacks fought for the Allied forces during World War II, most served in segregated units and received little thanks for their duty when they returned home. Many activists questioned how the U.S. government could claim to fight for freedom in foreign countries while millions of its own citizens were granted second-class rights at home. Cold War ideology and politics, therefore, also played major roles in securing equal rights for blacks.

Finally, the civil rights movement itself had an enormous, broad impact on domestic legislation, especially during Lyndon B. Johnson's presidency in the 1960s. In addition to calling for social equality, many civil rights leaders drew attention to the fact that the nation's poorest residents were mostly black. This reality, coupled with his predecessor John F. Kennedy's support of the civil rights movement, left Johnson with little choice but to act. The Civil Rights Act of 1964, which Johnson worked hard to push through Congress, included provisions to outlaw discrimination based not only on race but also on religion, nationality, or gender. The last provision contributed great momentum to the burgeoning feminist movement. Moreover, Johnson's later social policies, such as the War on Poverty and the Great Society, were effectively outgrowths of the movement for racial equality. Therefore, although the civil rights movement itself lost focus and dissipated in the 1970s, the effects of its concrete achievements have endured, not only for blacks but for other marginalized groups in American society as well.

SUMMARY OF EVENTS

A Hundred-Year Struggle

Black Americans' quest for official racial equality began the moment **Reconstruction** ended in the late 1870s. Even though Radical Republicans had attempted to aid blacks by passing the **Civil Rights Act of 1866**, the **Ku Klux Klan Act**, the **Civil Rights Act of 1875**, as well as the **Fourteenth Amendment** and **Fifteenth Amendment**, racist whites in the South ensured that blacks remained "in their place." The **black codes**, for example, as well as literacy tests, poll taxes, and widespread violence kept blacks away from voting booths, while conservative Supreme Court decisions ruined any chances for social equality. The **Compromise of 1877** effectively doomed southern blacks to a life of **sharecropping** and second-class citizenship.

The Early Movement

In 1896, in the landmark *Plessy v. Ferguson* decision, the conservative Supreme Court upheld the racist policy of segregation by legalizing **"separate but equal"** facilities for blacks and whites. In doing so, the court condemned blacks to more than a half century more of social inequality. Black leaders nonetheless continued to press for equal rights. For example, **Booker T. Washington**, president of the all-black **Tuskegee Institute** in Alabama, encouraged African Americans first to become self-sufficient economically before challenging whites on social issues. **W. E. B. Du Bois**, a Harvard-educated black historian and sociologist, however, ridiculed Washington's beliefs and argued that blacks should fight for social and economic equality all at once. Du Bois also hoped that blacks would eventually develop a **"black consciousness"** and cherish their distinctive history and cultural attributes. In 1910, he also helped found the **National Association for the Advancement of Colored People (NAACP)** to challenge the *Plessy* decision in the courtroom.

The Great Migration and Harlem Renaissance

Between World War I and World War II, more than a million blacks traveled from the South to the North in search of jobs, in what became known as the **Great Migration**. The **Harlem** neighborhood of New York City quickly became the nation's black cultural capital and housed one of the country's largest African-American communities, of approximately 200,000 people. Even though most of Harlem's residents were poor, during the 1920s, a small middle class emerged, consisting of poets, writers, and musicians. Artists and writers such as **Langston Hughes** and **Zora Neale Hurston** championed the **"New Negro,"** the African American who took pride in his or her cultural heritage. The flowering of black artistic and intellectual culture during this period became known as the **Harlem Renaissance**.

MARCUS GARVEY
Meanwhile, **Marcus Garvey**, a Jamaican immigrant and businessman, worked hard to promote black pride and nationalism. He founded the **Universal Negro Improvement Association**, which emphasized economic self-sufficiency as a means to overcome white dominance. He also encouraged blacks to leave the United States and resettle in Africa. Although most of Garvey's business ventures failed and he was eventually deported back to Jamaica, his message influenced many future civil rights leaders.

WORLD WAR II
More than a million black men served in the Allied forces during **World War II**, mostly in segregated noncombat units. At home, black leaders continued to push for racial equality and campaigned for the **"Double V"**—victory both at home and abroad. In 1941, **A. Philip Randolph**, the president of the **National Negro Congress**, threatened to lead thousands of black protesters in a march on Washington to demand the passage of more civil rights legislation. President **Franklin Delano Roosevelt**, afraid that the march might disrupt the war effort, compromised by signing **Executive Order 8802** to desegregate war factories and create the **Fair Employment Practices Committee**. As a result, more than 200,000 blacks were able to find top jobs in defense-related industries. After the war, President **Harry S Truman** created the **President's Committee on Civil Rights** and desegregated the military with **Executive Order 9981**.

BROWN V. BOARD OF EDUCATION
In 1954, after decades of legal work, **Thurgood Marshall**, the NAACP's chief counsel, finally managed to overturn the "separate but equal" doctrine (established in *Plessy v. Ferguson*) in ***Brown v. Board of Education of Topeka, Kansas***. Sympathetic Supreme Court chief justice **Earl Warren** convinced his fellow justices to declare unanimously that segregated public schools were inherently unequal. The *Brown* decision outraged conservative southern politicians in Congress, who protested it by drafting the **Southern Manifesto**.

THE LITTLE ROCK CRISIS

In 1957, Arkansas governor **Orval Faubus** chose to ignore a federal court order to desegregate the state's public schools and used the **National Guard** to prevent nine black students from entering **Central High School** in Little Rock. Although President **Dwight D. Eisenhower** personally opposed the *Brown* decision, he sent federal troops to integrate the high school by force and uphold federal supremacy over the state.

MARTIN LUTHER KING JR.

In 1955, the modern **civil rights movement** was effectively launched with the arrest of young seamstress **Rosa Parks** in Montgomery, Alabama. Police arrested Parks because she refused to give up her seat to a white man on a Montgomery city bus. After the arrest, blacks throughout the city joined together in a massive rally outside one of the city's Baptist churches to hear the young preacher **Martin Luther King Jr.** speak out against segregation, Parks's arrest, and the **Jim Crow** law she had violated. Blacks also organized the **Montgomery bus boycott**, boycotting city transportation for nearly a year before the Supreme Court finally struck down the city's segregated bus seating as unconstitutional.

In 1957, King formed the **Southern Christian Leadership Conference (SCLC)** to rally support from southern churches for the civil rights movement. Inspired by Indian political activist **Mohandas Gandhi**, King hoped the SCLC would lead a large-scale protest movement based on "love and nonviolence."

THE STUDENT MOVEMENT

Although the SCLC failed to initiate mass protest, a new student group called the **Student Nonviolent Coordinating Committee (SNCC)** accomplished much. The SNCC was launched in 1960 after the highly successful student-led **Greensboro sit-in** in North Carolina and went on to coordinate peaceful student protests against segregation throughout the South. The students also helped the **Congress of Racial Equality (CORE)** organize **Freedom Rides** throughout the Deep South. In 1961, groups of both black and white **Freedom Riders** boarded interstate buses, hoping to provoke violence, get the attention of the federal government, and win the sympathy of more moderate whites. The plan worked: angry white mobs attacked Freedom Riders in Alabama so many times that several riders nearly died. Still, many of the students believed that the media attention they had received had been worth the price.

THE BIRMINGHAM PROTEST

The overwhelming public support from the North for Freedom Riders prompted Martin Luther King Jr. to launch more peaceful protests, hoping to anger die-hard segregationists. In 1963, King focused all of his energy on organizing a massive protest in the heavily segregated city of **Birmingham**, Alabama. Thousands of blacks participated in the rally, including several hundred local high school students who marched in their own **"children's crusade."** Birmingham's commissioner, **"Bull" Connor**, cracked down on the protesters using clubs, vicious police dogs, and water cannons. King was arrested along with hundreds of others and used his time in jail to write his famous **"Letter from Birmingham Jail"** to explain the civil rights movement to critics.

KENNEDY AND THE MARCH ON WASHINGTON

The violence during the Birmingham protest shocked northerners even more than the violence of the Freedom Rides and convinced President **John F. Kennedy** to risk his own political future and fully endorse the civil rights movement. Meanwhile, in 1963, King and the SCLC joined forces with CORE, the NAACP, and the SNCC in organizing the **March on Washington** in August. More than 200,000 blacks and whites participated in the march, one of the largest political rallies in American history. The highlight of the rally was King's sermonic **"I have a dream" speech**.

FEDERAL HELP

Kennedy was assassinated in November 1963, but the new president, **Lyndon B. Johnson**, honored his predecessor's commitment to the civil rights movement. Johnson actually had opposed the movement while serving as Senate majority leader but changed his mind because he wanted to establish himself as the leader of a united Democratic Party. He therefore pressured Congress to pass the **Civil Rights Act of 1964**, an even tougher bill than Kennedy had hoped would pass. The act outlawed discrimination and segregation based on race, nationality, or gender.

The same year, the **Twenty-Fourth Amendment** to the U.S. Constitution was ratified, outlawing poll taxes as a prerequisite for voting in federal elections. Furthermore, SNCC activists traveled to Mississippi that summer on the **Freedom Summer** campaign to register more black voters, again hoping their actions would provoke segregationist whites.

THE VOTING RIGHTS ACT

Violent opposition to the Freedom Summer campaign convinced Martin Luther King Jr. that more attention needed to be drawn to the fact that few southern blacks were actually able to exercise their right to vote. Springing into action, King traveled to the small town of **Selma**, Alabama, in 1965, to support a local protest against racial restrictions at the polls. There, he joined thousands of blacks peacefully trying to register to vote. Police, however, attacked the protesters on **"Bloody Sunday,"** killing several activists in the most violent crackdown yet. The same year, an outraged Lyndon B. Johnson and Congress responded by passing the **Voting Rights Act** to safeguard blacks' right to vote. The act outlawed literacy tests and sent thousands of federal voting officials into the South to supervise black **voter registration**.

MALCOLM X AND THE NATION OF ISLAM

However, a growing number of black activists had begun to oppose integration altogether by the mid-1960s. **Malcolm X** of the **Nation of Islam** was the most vocal critic of King's nonviolent tactics. Instead, Malcolm X preached black self-sufficiency, just as Marcus Garvey had four decades earlier. He also advocated armed self-defense against white oppression, arguing that bloodshed was necessary for revolution. However, Malcolm X left the Nation of Islam after numerous scandals hit the organization, and he traveled to Mecca, Saudi Arabia, on a religious pilgrimage in 1964. In the course of his journey, he encountered Muslims of all nationalities who challenged his belief system and forced him to rethink his opinions regarding race relations. When Malcolm X returned to the United States, he joined forces with the SNCC in the nonviolent fight against segregation and racism. However, he was assassinated in early 1965.

BLACK POWER

Despite Malcolm X's untimely death, his original message of race separation (instead of integration) lived on and inspired many students in the SNCC, who also expressed dissatisfaction with the gains made through peaceful protests. Although the Civil Rights Act and Voting Rights Act were landmark laws for the civil rights movement, young activists such as **Stokely Carmichael** felt they had not done enough to correct centuries of inequality. In 1967, Carmichael argued in his book ***Black Power*** that blacks should take pride in their heritage and culture and should not have anything to do with whites in the United States or anywhere else. In fact, Carmichael even promoted one plan to split the United States into separate black and white countries.

THE BLACK PANTHERS

Frustrated activists in Oakland, California, responded to Stokely Carmichael's "black power" theories and formed the **Black Panther Party for Self-Defense**. The Black Panthers, armed and clad in black, operated basic social services in the urban ghettos, patrolled the streets, and called for an armed revolution. Although the Black Panthers did provide valuable support to the community, their embrace of violence prompted a massive government crackdown on the group, leading to its dissolution in the late 1960s and early 1970s.

THE COLLAPSE OF THE MOVEMENT

Black revolutionaries such as Malcolm X, Stokely Carmichael, and the Black Panthers, along with the scores of **race riots** that rocked America between 1965 and 1970, frightened many white Americans and alienated many moderates who had supported peaceful protest. President Lyndon B. Johnson had also become suspicious of civil rights activists and ordered the FBI to begin investigations of Malcolm X, the Nation of Islam, and even Martin Luther King Jr. himself for their alleged ties to **Communist** organizations. Then, in 1968, a young white man named **James Earl Ray** shot and killed King as he addressed a crowd gathered in Memphis, Tennessee. King's death, combined with the increasing amount of violence, effectively ended the civil rights movement of the 1950s and 1960s.

The momentum seemed to slow w/ King's death

KEY PEOPLE & TERMS

PEOPLE

STOKELY CARMICHAEL
Black leader who called for independence, self-reliance, and black nationalism in his 1967 book *Black Power*. Carmichael became tired of the **Student Nonviolent Coordinating Committee**'s theory of "love and nonviolence" and expelled its white members in 1966. He condoned the use of violence to achieve revolution and independence and even envisioned splitting the United States into separate black and white countries.

W. E. B. DU BOIS
Harvard-educated black historian and sociologist who pushed for both equal economic and social rights for African Americans in the late nineteenth and early twentieth centuries. Du Bois disagreed with other black leaders, such as **Booker T. Washington**, who fought only for economic equality. Du Bois also worked to develop a **"black consciousness,"** promoting black history, religious heritage, art, music, and culture. He also helped found the **NAACP** in 1909.

DWIGHT D. EISENHOWER
The least supportive president of the civil rights movement in the mid–twentieth century. Eisenhower refused to endorse or comment publicly on the Supreme Court's decision in *Brown v. Board of Education* and even privately admitted that he regretted appointing Chief Justice **Earl Warren** to the bench. Although Eisenhower did dispatch federal troops to oversee the integration of **Central High School** during the **Little Rock crisis,** he did so only because Arkansas governor **Orval Faubus** had defied a federal court order, not because he believed in integration. Moreover, Eisenhower had also opposed President Truman's **Executive Order 9981** to desegregate the armed forces in 1948. Eisenhower did sign the **Civil Rights Act of 1957,** but only as a political gesture and only after assuring southerners that the act would have little impact on day-to-day life.

MARCUS GARVEY
A Jamaican immigrant and black activist who promoted **black nationalism** and the idea of the **"New Negro"** in black communities

9

in New York during the **Harlem Renaissance** of the 1920s. Garvey's **Universal Negro Improvement Association** encouraged blacks to become independent and self-sufficient and to do more business within the black community. He also led a movement to resettle blacks in Africa. In 1927, however, the federal government deported Garvey after he was indicted on charges of mail fraud. Still, his message influenced future black leaders, including **Elijah Muhammad**, **Malcolm X**, and **Stokely Carmichael**.

LYNDON B. JOHNSON

Thirty-sixth U.S. president and one of the civil rights movement's greatest supporters after he assumed the presidency in 1963. Even though Johnson had opposed the movement in the 1940s and 1950s, he changed his mind and decided to use the issue of civil rights to establish himself as the leader of the Democratic Party in the wake of **John F. Kennedy**'s assassination. Johnson also hoped to stem the racial violence in the South before it intensified beyond his control. He therefore pressured Congress to pass an even more potent civil rights bill than Kennedy had asked for in 1963. Thanks to an enormous effort on Johnson's part, Congress passed the **Civil Rights Act of 1964** and the **Voting Rights Act** in 1965. Ironically, Johnson later ordered the FBI to investigate Martin Luther King Jr. and Malcolm X for suspected ties to Communist organizations.

JOHN F. KENNEDY

Thirty-fifth U.S. president and a leading supporter of the civil rights movement. Even though black voters helped him win the election in 1960, Kennedy supported the civil rights movement only tacitly during his first two years in office. He feared that more explicit support on his part would alienate conservative southern Democrats in Congress. The violence of the **Birmingham campaign**, however, convinced Kennedy to endorse the civil rights movement publicly, even at the risk of losing the next election. He had plans to push a stronger civil rights bill through Congress but was assassinated in 1963.

MARTIN LUTHER KING JR.

A civil rights leader during the 1950s and 1960s who fought to protect the rights of blacks in the South. King rose to national fame after he took charge of the **Montgomery bus boycott** in 1955. An amazing speaker, he quickly became the de facto leader of the civil rights movement. He hoped to desegregate the South and protect blacks' political rights through "love and nonviolence" and peaceful protest. In 1957, he founded the **Southern Christian Leadership Conference (SCLC)** to rally southern churches behind the movement. On countless occasions, he purposefully incited violence by racist southerners against blacks in order to win sympathy from moderate white Americans. A talented writer, King penned many of the finest essays about the movement, including his 1963 **"Letter from Birmingham Jail."** He received the **Nobel Peace Prize** in 1964, which boosted global awareness of the civil rights movement and put pressure on the federal government to address racial inequality in the United States. However, King's efforts were cut short when he was assassinated by **James Earl Ray** in Memphis in 1968.

THURGOOD MARSHALL

Chief counsel for the **NAACP** who worked to rid America of the "separate but equal" doctrine that the Supreme Court had upheld in the 1896 *Plessy v. Ferguson* ruling. Marshall won key victories in *Morgan v. Virginia* (1946) and *Sweatt v. Painter* (1950), but his greatest achievement was convincing the Warren Court to overturn *Plessy v. Ferguson* in the *Brown v. Board of Education of Topeka, Kansas*, decision (1954). Marshall later went on to become the first African-American justice on the U.S. Supreme Court.

ROSA PARKS

A college-educated seamstress who effectively launched the first peaceful protest of the civil rights movement. The peaceful protest began when Parks boarded a Montgomery, Alabama, city bus on December 1, 1955, and refused to give up her seat to a white man who was looking for a seat because the "white" section was full. Police arrested her for defying the city's law, prompting outraged blacks to start the **Montgomery bus boycott** later that year.

EARL WARREN

Supreme Court justice appointed by conservative president **Dwight D. Eisenhower** in 1953. Warren proved to be surprisingly liberal during his tenure as chief justice. He fully supported the quest of many blacks to end racial segregation, for example, and worked hard to get the Court to deliver a unanimous verdict in *Brown v. Board of Education* to overturn the "separate but equal" doctrine in 1954.

BOOKER T. WASHINGTON

President of the **Tuskegee Institute** in Alabama who pushed blacks to achieve economic equality with whites. Washington did not advocate immediate social equality but rather believed that economic equality would eventually bring social equality. Other black leaders, such as **W. E. B. Du Bois**, disagreed sharply with Washington's views.

MALCOLM X

Prominent civil rights leader who quickly became the national voice for the black nationalist **Nation of Islam** in the early 1950s. The son of a civil rights leader, Malcolm Little converted to Islam while serving a prison term in the 1940s. He then changed his surname to "X" to represent the heritage and identity of the black people lost during centuries of slavery. A dynamic speaker, Malcolm X espoused self-reliance, militancy, and independence for blacks, in contrast to **Martin Luther King Jr.**'s doctrine of love, nonviolence, and integration. Malcolm X's view of the civil rights movement changed, however, while he was on a holy pilgrimage to Mecca in 1964. When he returned, he broke away from with the Nation of Islam and, with nonviolent organizations such as the SNCC, began working toward racial integration. In a tragic turn of events, rivals within the Nation of Islam assassinated him in 1965. Although his career was cut short, Malcolm X's early views and opinions greatly influenced the **"black power" movement** that began in the late 1960s.

TERMS

BIRMINGHAM CAMPAIGN

A peaceful protest organized by **Martin Luther King Jr.** and the **SCLC** in Birmingham, Alabama. By protesting, King hoped to provoke violent reactions by racist whites and win national media attention. The tactic worked, as city commissioner **"Bull" Connor** ordered police to use force to end the protest, and northern whites watched the violence unfold on national television. While serving a short jail sentence in Birmingham, King wrote his famous **"Letter from Birmingham Jail,"** in which he explained the civil rights movement to his critics. The Birmingham campaign also convinced President **John F. Kennedy** to endorse the movement fully and pressure Congress to pass more civil rights legislation.

BLACK PANTHERS

An organization of militant black civil rights activists inspired by **Stokely Carmichael**'s **"black power"** philosophies. The Black Panther Party for Self-Defense formed in Oakland, California, in 1966. Armed and clad entirely in black, Black Panther militants advocated the use of violence to incite a racial revolution in the United States. In addition to fomenting rebellion, they helped poor residents in black communities by running clinics and schools. The party disbanded, however, following an intense U.S. government crackdown in the late 1960s.

BLACK POWER

A term coined by militant former **SNCC** leader **Stokely Carmichael**. The black power movement reflected the growing push for militancy, self-reliance, independence, and nationalism within the black community and civil rights movement in the late 1960s and early 1970s.

BROWN V. BOARD OF EDUCATION OF TOPEKA, KANSAS

A Supreme Court ruling that desegregated public schools. The **NAACP**'s chief counsel, **Thurgood Marshall**, won a major victory for black Americans when he convinced the Supreme Court to hear *Brown v. Board of Education of Topeka, Kansas*, in 1954. Chief Justice **Earl Warren**, who supported desegregation, then convinced the justices to hand down a unanimous ruling that overturned the "separate but equal" doctrine the Court had established in *Plessy v. Ferguson* sixty years earlier. President **Dwight D. Eisenhower** personally opposed the decision and therefore refused to comment on the ruling or endorse the blossoming civil rights movement.

CIVIL RIGHTS ACT OF 1957

An act that nominally outlawed racial segregation and created a civil rights division within the Justice Department. Congress passed the act in the wake of the **Montgomery bus boycott** and the **Little Rock crisis**. However, the act had more of a symbolic impact than a legal one; President **Dwight D. Eisenhower** signed the bill only reluctantly and assured southern politicians that the law would not bring about any major changes in daily life.

CIVIL RIGHTS ACT OF 1964

An act that outlawed discrimination in public places and the workplace on the basis of race, religion, nationality, or gender. The act also created the **Equal Employment Opportunity Commission (EEOC)** to ensure that people would abide by the law. President **Lyndon B.**

Johnson used all his political power to push the bill through Congress, because he knew the bill would allow him to take control of the divided Democratic Party. Interestingly, the incorporation of the word *gender* into the law helped the **feminist movement** gain momentum in the late 1960s.

Congress of Racial Equality (CORE)

An organization founded in 1942 to campaign against segregation in the North using sit-ins and other nonviolent forms of protest. CORE later worked closely with the **SNCC**, the **SCLC**, and the **NAACP** to organize nonviolent rallies and protests such as the **Freedom Rides** and the **March on Washington**.

Freedom Rides

A series of protests aimed at the desegregation of buses in the South. Beginning in 1961, **CORE** and the **SNCC** organized several interracial Freedom Rides to win sympathy from whites in the North by provoking racist southerners. **Freedom Riders** met violent mobs throughout Alabama who burned buses and nearly beat several of the riders to death. Southern police also arrested riders for inciting violence and disturbing the peace.

Freedom Summer

An **SNCC**-sponsored event that sent nearly 1,000 people—mostly young, white student volunteers from the North—to Mississippi in 1964 to provoke southern white ire. Volunteers helped register tens of thousands of black voters, formed the **Mississippi Freedom Democratic Party**, and taught civic classes to poor blacks. Unfortunately, these volunteers paid a heavy price: hundreds were arrested, scores were stabbed and shot, and several died in their efforts to empower black Mississippians. The **Freedom Summer** campaign helped convince the U.S. Congress to ratify the **Twenty-Fourth Amendment** and pass the **Civil Rights Act of 1964**.

Greensboro Sit-In

A 1960 protest in which four black college students sat at an all-white lunch counter in a Woolworth's store in **Greensboro**, North Carolina, and demanded service. When the clerks refused, the students continued to sit quietly at the counter and refused to leave. The students returned each subsequent day with additional supporters until hundreds of people had joined them. City officials eventually agreed to desegregate Woolworth's and other local stores, but only after blacks had waged a long and costly boycott.

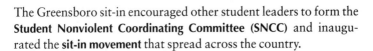

The Greensboro sit-in encouraged other student leaders to form the **Student Nonviolent Coordinating Committee (SNCC)** and inaugurated the **sit-in movement** that spread across the country.

JIM CROW LAWS

A term for racist laws and social orders in the South that kept blacks separate from and subordinate to whites. The Jim Crow laws that appeared after the *Plessy v. Ferguson* ruling of 1896 forced blacks to sit, eat, sleep, study, and work in separate facilities (although these Jim Crow laws were not as harsh as the **black codes** of the Reconstruction era). In 1955, **Rosa Parks** challenged one of the Jim Crow laws of Montgomery, Alabama, when she refused to give up her bus seat to a white man. Blacks went on to protest these laws effectively with boycotts and sit-ins during the civil rights movement. The federal government also helped the movement with the passage of the **Civil Rights Act in 1964**.

LITTLE ROCK CRISIS

A crisis that occurred in 1957 when the governor of Arkansas, **Orval Faubus**, defied a federal court order to integrate public high schools in the state and federal troops were sent in to enforce the law. In the hopes of winning votes from his white constituents, Faubus flouted the law and ordered the **Arkansas National Guard** to prevent nine black students from entering **Central High School** in the state's capital, Little Rock. President **Dwight D. Eisenhower**, though not a supporter of the civil rights movement, placed the National Guard under federal authority and sent 1,000 army troops to escort the students to class and uphold U.S. law.

MARCH ON WASHINGTON

One of the largest political rallies in American history, during which more than 200,000 blacks and whites gathered in front of the **Lincoln Memorial** in Washington, D.C., on August 28, 1963, to demonstrate their support for more civil rights legislation from Congress. Empowered by their success in Birmingham, **SCLC** leaders joined forces with the **SNCC**, **CORE**, and the **NAACP** in organizing the march. **Martin Luther King Jr.** ended the rally with his famous **"I have a dream" speech**.

MONTGOMERY BUS BOYCOTT

A yearlong boycott beginning in 1955 in which blacks avoided city transportation in **Montgomery**, Alabama, to protest the arrest of **Rosa Parks** for refusing to give up her bus seat to a white man. **Martin**

Luther King Jr. became a national figure when he took charge of the boycott and protest. The Supreme Court ended the boycott the following year, forcing the city of Montgomery to desegregate public transportation.

NATIONAL ASSOCIATION FOR THE ADVANCEMENT OF COLORED PEOPLE (NAACP)

An organization founded by **W. E. B. Du Bois** and several white northerners that sought to achieve legal victories for blacks, especially the reversal of the **"separate but equal"** doctrine established by the Supreme Court in the 1896 *Plessy v. Ferguson* decision. After decades of legal battles, the NAACP's top lawyer, **Thurgood Marshall**, finally achieved several victories, including *Morgan v. Virginia*, *McLaurin v. Oklahoma State Regents*, and *Sweatt v. Painter*. The NAACP's greatest victory, however, came when the Supreme Court reversed *Plessy v. Ferguson* with the ***Brown v. Board of Education of Topeka, Kansas***, ruling in 1954.

NATION OF ISLAM

A group founded in 1930 to promote **black nationalism** in Detroit's black community during the **Great Depression**. Under the early leadership of **Elijah Muhammad**, the organization appealed to the poorest urban blacks and quickly spread to the major cities in the East. **Malcolm X** emerged as the organization's chief spokesman in the early 1950s and continued to push for black independence from whites and self-reliance in daily life. The Nation of Islam also operated many stores in urban black neighborhoods throughout America to promote black economic independence.

SELMA CAMPAIGN

A black voter–registration drive in the small town of **Selma**, Alabama, that became a focal point for the civil rights movement in 1965. When police attacked thousands of peaceful black protesters petitioning the government for the right to vote, national controversy ensued. **"Bloody Sunday,"** as the incident came to be called, shocked northerners, Congress, and President **Lyndon B. Johnson**, who asked Congress to help protect black voting rights. Congress complied and passed the **Voting Rights Act** in 1965.

SOUTHERN CHRISTIAN LEADERSHIP CONFERENCE (SCLC)

A coalition founded in 1957 by **Martin Luther King Jr.** and nearly one hundred other southern ministers to rally church support for the blossoming civil rights movement. King and other SCLC leaders preached a way to integrate black and white America through **"love and nonviolence."** Although the SCLC did not launch the widespread peaceful protest movement that King originally envisioned, it did play a prominent role in most of the nonviolent campaigns that took place between 1957 and 1965.

Student Nonviolent Coordinating Committee (SNCC)
A civil rights organization founded in 1960, after the highly successful **Greensboro sit-in**, whose goal was to organize students on campuses across the country. The SNCC was one of the most active groups of the civil rights movement and participated in nearly every major peaceful campaign. Ironically, disillusioned SNCC members such as **Stokely Carmichael** formulated the philosophy of **"black power"** to advocate violence in order to break away from white society rather than bring about peaceful integration.

Twenty-Fourth Amendment
An amendment to the U.S. Constitution that outlawed the payment of **poll taxes** as a prerequisite for voting in federal elections. The Twenty-Fourth Amendment was ratified in 1964.

Voting Rights Act
A 1965 act that outlawed literacy tests as a voting prerequisite and sent federal election officials into the South to help blacks register to vote. Congress passed the act partly in response to racial violence in **Selma**, Alabama. Because the new law drastically increased the percentage of black voters in the South, some historians have claimed that it marked the true end of **Reconstruction**, which had begun exactly one hundred years earlier.

Watts Riots
Violent riots that occurred in the Watts neighborhood of **Los Angeles** in 1965. For six days, more than 50,000 black residents rioted to protest poverty, racism, and continued unemployment. It took 20,000 National Guardsmen to end the riots, and more than thirty people died in the mayhem.

KEY PEOPLE & TERMS

SUMMARY & ANALYSIS

THE FAILURE OF RECONSTRUCTION: 1877–1900

EVENTS

1866	Congress passes Civil Rights Act of 1866
1868	Fourteenth Amendment is ratified
1870	Fifteenth Amendment is ratified
1871	Congress passes Ku Klux Klan Act
1875	Congress passes Civil Rights Act of 1875
1877	Reconstruction ends
1881	Booker T. Washington founds Tuskegee Institute
1896	*Plessy v. Ferguson* ruling upholds "separate but equal" doctrine

KEY PEOPLE

W. E. B. Du Bois Black historian and sociologist; pushed for equal economic and social rights and worked to develop "black consciousness" by promoting black culture and heritage

Booker T. Washington President of Tuskegee Institute; campaigned for blacks to achieve economic equality with whites; thought blacks should pursue economic equality first, before social equality

SAFEGUARDING BLACKS' RIGHTS

After the **Civil War** ended in 1865, Radical Republicans in Congress attempted to protect blacks' rights by passing the **Civil Rights Act of 1866**, which enabled blacks to file lawsuits against whites and sit on juries. To safeguard these rights permanently, states ratified the **Fourteenth Amendment** and enfranchised black men with the **Fifteenth Amendment**.

Congress also passed the **Ku Klux Klan Act** of 1871, which outlawed racial terrorism, and the **Civil Rights Act of 1875**, which prohibited racial discrimination in most public places. Radical Republicans also tried to use the **Freedmen's Bureau** to redistribute confiscated southern plantation lands to blacks in order to put them on more equal footing with white farmers. In addition to these measures, Congress sent federal troops into the South to help blacks register to vote.

THE FAILURE OF RECONSTRUCTION

However, opposition from President **Andrew Johnson**, a conservative Supreme Court, and the white southern elite thwarted Radical Republicans' attempts at protecting blacks' rights. Johnson, for example, disbanded the Freedmen's Bureau, and the Supreme Court declared the **Civil Rights Act of 1875** unconstitutional. Then, in the complex maneuvering of the **Compromise of 1877**, Republicans traded the presidency (the election of Rutherford B. Hayes) for the premature withdrawal of federal troops from the South. This compromise effectively ended Reconstruction and set back the hope of equality for southern blacks for decades. Within a few short years, the powerful white elite had returned to power in southern legislatures and had reinstated its racist policies in the South.

SHARECROPPING AND THE BLACK CODES

During the last decades of the 1800s, life for southern blacks was harsh. By 1880, most blacks had become **sharecroppers**, tenant farmers who essentially rented land from their former masters. Even though most former slaves actually preferred the sharecropping system to wage labor, it kept them bound to their white landlords in virtual slavery.

In addition, local statutes called **black codes** kept blacks "in their place." These laws made "offenses" such as loitering, unemployment, indebtedness, voting, and even having sex with white women illegal for blacks. State authorities fined and arrested blacks who disobeyed these laws, so the codes effectively made racism legal. Moreover, the black codes gave the white supremacist **Ku Klux Klan** even more of a motive and opportunity to terrorize blacks. As a result, almost all southern blacks at the time lived in abject poverty and had virtually no social or political rights.

RACIAL DARWINISM

Although northern blacks enjoyed more rights than southern blacks, they still suffered from severe racial prejudice. One South Carolina politician who believed in the "natural" racial superiority of whites claimed that the average black American was "a fiend, a wild beast, seeking whom he may devour." Another social commentator likened blacks to wild animals that operated only on instinct. It is therefore not surprising that most blacks even in the North were able to obtain only unskilled jobs and lived in some of the poorest neighborhoods.

BOOKER T. WASHINGTON AND ACCOMMODATION

The few educated blacks in the South, however, strove to change the status quo. In 1881, former slave **Booker T. Washington**, for example, founded a technical college in Alabama for blacks, called the **Tuskegee Institute**. Washington quickly became one of the first black activists as he called on blacks to achieve economic equality with whites. A proponent of **"accommodation,"** Washington argued that social equality and political rights would come only if blacks first became self-reliant and improved their financial footing. Then, he argued, respect from the white community would naturally follow. On the other hand, Washington privately worked to improve blacks' social standing, despite his publicly stated belief that "agitation of questions of social equality is the extremist folly." He helped push for an end to segregation, for example, and supported organizations bent on securing political rights for more blacks.

W. E. B. DU BOIS AND THE BLACK CONSCIOUSNESS

Many black activists in the North, however, disagreed with Washington. His policy of accommodation, they argued, doomed blacks to an eternity of poverty and second-class citizenship. Leaders such as **W. E. B. Du Bois** called for blacks to seek complete and immediate social *and* economic equality. Du Bois also called on blacks to develop a **"black consciousness"** distinctive from that of whites. In his seminal 1903 book *The Souls of Black Folk*, he argued that blacks needed to become more aware of their history, art, music, and religious backgrounds in order to understand themselves fully.

PLESSY V. FERGUSON

The Supreme Court's *Plessy v. Ferguson* decision in 1896 was a major setback for early civil rights activists. The decision declared that segregated public and private facilities for blacks and whites were **"separate but equal,"** effectively justifying **Jim Crow** segregation laws. The single justice who opposed the decision astutely remarked that the *Plessy v. Ferguson* decision would set back African Americans' struggle for equality by decades. Just as significant, the Court also upheld the right of southern legislatures to levy poll taxes and give literacy tests—strategies that were meant to exclude blacks from voting. These decisions effectively legalized and spread racism throughout the North and South.

TWENTIETH-CENTURY ROOTS:
1900–1950

EVENTS

1909	NAACP is founded
1920	Great Migration begins
1927	Marcus Garvey is deported
1941	Roosevelt signs Executive Order 8802, creates Fair Employment Practices Committee
1942	CORE is founded
1946	Truman creates Committee on Civil Rights
1947	Jackie Robinson becomes first black player in Major League Baseball
1948	Executive Order 9981 signed
1950	Ralph Bunche wins Nobel Peace Prize

KEY PEOPLE

W. E. B. Du Bois Black historian and sociologist; helped found the NAACP in 1909

Marcus Garvey Jamaican immigrant who promoted "black nationalism"; helped found UNIA; led movement to resettle blacks in Africa

A. Philip Randolph President of National Negro Congress; threatened to march on Washington during World War II if more civil rights legislation was not passed

Franklin D. Roosevelt 32nd U.S. president; signed Executive Order 8802 and created Fair Practices Employment Committee

Harry S Truman 33rd U.S. president; created President's Committee on Civil Rights and signed Executive Order 9981 to desegregate U.S. military

Jackie Robinson Athlete who in 1947 became first black player in Major League Baseball

Ralph Bunche U.N. diplomat who in 1950 became first African American to win Nobel Peace Prize

THE NAACP

In 1909, **W. E. B. Du Bois** and several other activists, frustrated by setbacks to the civil rights movement such as *Plessy v. Ferguson*, founded the **National Association for the Advancement of Colored People (NAACP)**. The NAACP, whose leadership and membership consisted of both blacks and whites, published a monthly journal called *Crisis* and worked diligently to gain more legal and political rights for blacks.

Black women, meanwhile, formed their own associations geared toward providing social services and community support. The **National Association of Colored Women's Clubs**, for example, worked to improve the lives of urban black women by building settlement houses, promoting public health initiatives, and providing child-care services for working mothers.

SUMMARY & ANALYSIS

THE GREAT MIGRATION

The prospect of new jobs in the war industries encouraged as many as half a million black tenant farmers in the South to move to cities in the North during and after World War I. The **Great Migration**, as it came to be called, had a profound effect on blacks' lives and on the cities in which they resettled, as millions of white Americans began leaving for the suburbs. Furthermore, the invention of the mechanical cotton picker in the 1940s made southern agricultural jobs scarcer and spurred more than a million additional blacks to leave the South. As more and more blacks moved to northern cities, more people became aware of the enormous economic inequalities that separated blacks from whites.

THE HARLEM RENAISSANCE

Nowhere were the effects of the Great Migration clearer than in the **Harlem** neighborhood of New York City, where as many as 200,000 blacks settled between World War I and World War II. Harlem quickly became one of the largest black communities in the world outside Africa. Although most of the blacks who moved to Harlem lived in poverty, a sizable group of middle-class blacks helped lead the so-called **Harlem Renaissance** of the 1920s.

During this Harlem Renaissance, W. E. B. Du Bois's "black consciousness" took root among black artists and intellectuals, who began to recognize, develop, and appreciate a distinctive black cultural identity. Black writers such as **Zora Neale Hurston, Claude McKay, Countee Cullen,** and **Langston Hughes** expressed their immense pride in the creation of the **"New Negro."** As black essayist **James Weldon Johnson** put it, "Nothing can go further to destroy race prejudice than the recognition of the Negro as a creator and contributor to American civilization."

MARCUS GARVEY AND THE UNIA

No single individual contributed more to the development of black pride during this period than **Marcus Garvey**. Garvey, who founded the **Universal Negro Improvement Association (UNIA)** in Jamaica in 1914, moved to the United States in 1916. He settled in Harlem and established the U.S. branch of the UNIA to help blacks achieve economic independence in the United States and unite black communities around the world. He organized parades and massive rallies to boost black pride and encouraged black-owned companies to do more business within the community. On the other hand, the UNIA also encouraged blacks to leave the United States and resettle in their ancestral homes in **Africa**.

Even though most of Garvey's business ventures failed and the U.S. government deported him for mail fraud in 1927, his contribution to the development of black consciousness empowered the "New Negro" and helped lay the foundation for the civil rights movement in the 1950s and 1960s.

WORLD WAR II

The majority of the more than 1 million blacks who joined the Allied forces during World War II served in segregated, noncombat service and maintenance units, just as they had in World War I. There were exceptions, however, perhaps the most notable of which was the elite all-black **Tuskegee Airmen** bomber unit.

Segregated or not, black Americans made significant gains during the war. Civil rights leaders, for example, pushed their **"Double V"** campaign for both victory abroad and victory at home. NAACP membership soared during the war years to more than half a million people. The newly formed **Congress of Racial Equality (CORE)** launched peaceful protests in order to gain sympathy for the movement from white Americans. National Negro Congress President **A. Philip Randolph** even threatened President **Franklin D. Roosevelt** with a massive march on Washington, D.C., if the federal government failed to pass more civil rights legislation.

ROOSEVELT AND CIVIL RIGHTS

Hoping to avoid civil unrest, Roosevelt compromised with Randolph by signing **Executive Order 8802**, which outlawed racial discrimination in the federal government and in war factories. Roosevelt also established the **Fair Employment Practices Committee** to execute the order. As a result, more than 200,000 Northern blacks found work in defense-related industries during the war. Roosevelt's election victories during the Great Depression and World War II happened, in part, because a majority of black Americans began voting for Democrats rather than Republicans. Continued support from the Democratic Party proved to be vital in securing the passage of civil rights legislation in the 1960s.

TRUMAN AND CIVIL RIGHTS

After the war, in 1946, President **Harry S Truman** established the **President's Committee on Civil Rights**. The committee pushed for antilynching laws in the South and tried to register more black voters. Although symbolically powerful, the committee had little practical influence. More significant was Truman's desegregation of the armed forces with **Executive Order 9981** in 1948. Truman's support for civil rights angered many southerners within the Democratic Party, though, and many left the nominating convention in 1948 to back their own presidential candidate, segregationist **Strom Thurmond** of South Carolina.

NOTABLE FIRSTS

Two major color barriers were broken shortly after the war's end. The first was in 1947, when **Jackie Robinson** became the first black professional baseball player in the major leagues. Robinson's contract with the Brooklyn Dodgers opened professional sports to black players and helped integrate blacks into white American culture.

The second occurred in 1950, when United Nations diplomat **Ralph Bunche** became the first black man to win the prestigious Nobel Peace Prize for his work in reducing Arab-Israeli tensions. Although President Truman offered Bunche a promotion to the position of undersecretary of state, Bunche declined the offer after learning that he and his family would still have to live in the segregated black quarter of Washington, D.C.

EARLY LEGAL VICTORIES: 1938–1957

EVENTS

1938	*Missouri ex rel. Gaines v. Canada* ruling
1946	*Morgan v. Virginia* ruling
1950	*Sweatt v. Painter* and *McLaurin v. Oklahoma State Regents* rulings
1954	*Brown v. Board of Education of Topeka, Kansas*, ruling
1955	Montgomery bus boycott
1956	Several states issue Southern Manifesto in response to *Brown* decision
1957	Southern Christian Leadership Conference (SCLC) forms Civil Rights Act of 1957 passed by Congress Eisenhower intervenes in Little Rock crisis

KEY PEOPLE

Dwight D. Eisenhower 34th U.S. president; personally opposed civil rights movement but used military to resolve Little Rock crisis in 1957

Orval Faubus Arkansas governor who defied federal court order to integrate public high schools; ordered Arkansas National Guard to prevent black students from entering Central High School in Little Rock

Martin Luther King Jr. Preacher who gained prominence by leading Montgomery bus boycott in 1955; founded SCLC in 1957 to rally southern churches behind civil rights movement

Thurgood Marshall Chief counsel for NAACP; argued *Brown v. Board of Education* before Supreme Court in 1954

Earl Warren Supreme Court chief justice who proved unexpectedly liberal on civil rights; worked hard to deliver unanimous verdict on *Brown v. Board of Education*

Rosa Parks Seamstress who launched era of peaceful protest by refusing to give up her seat on a Montgomery, Alabama, city bus; her arrest prompted the Montgomery bus boycott later that year

THE LEGAL STRATEGY

The **NAACP**'s primary goal upon its founding in 1909 was to tackle racial inequality by means of legal action, hoping to overturn the "separate but equal" doctrine of *Plessy v. Ferguson*. One of the organization's earliest victories came in 1938, when the Supreme Court ruled in **Missouri ex rel. Gaines v. Canada** that the University of Missouri had to build an entirely new law school for blacks or simply integrate them into the existing all-white school.

In 1946, the Supreme Court further chipped away at the "separate but equal" doctrine when it ruled in **Morgan v. Virginia** that segregated interstate buses were illegal because they put an "undue burden" on interstate trade and transportation. In 1950, the court expanded on the *Missouri* decision when it ruled in **Sweatt v. Painter** that "separate but equal" professional schools were inherently unequal.

SUMMARY & ANALYSIS

THURGOOD MARSHALL

One of the main figures in the NAACP during this period of legal action was its chief counsel, **Thurgood Marshall**. A brilliant lawyer, Marshall won a major victory in 1950 with the *McLaurin v. Oklahoma State Regents* ruling, when he convinced the Supreme Court that segregated cafeterias, libraries, and seats in classrooms placed a "badge of inferiority" on black students. After winning several landmark victories, Marshall himself would go on to become the first black justice on the Supreme Court, in 1967.

BROWN V. BOARD OF EDUCATION

The early string of decisive legal victories for civil rights activists laid the foundation for Marshall and the NAACP to launch a head-on attack on the *Plessy v. Ferguson* decision. In 1951, they accepted the case of **Oliver Brown** of Topeka, Kansas, who wanted his daughter to be able to attend an all-white elementary school near his house rather than a black school several miles away. The case—*Brown v. Board of Education of Topeka, Kansas*—eventually worked its way up to the Supreme Court, where Marshall argued that racial segregation relegated black Americans to second-class citizenship. Chief Justice **Earl Warren**, though appointed by the conservative **Dwight D. Eisenhower**, sympathized with black Americans and pressured the wavering justices on the bench to vote in Brown's favor. Warren knew that only a unanimous decision would be powerful enough to quiet racists and truly overturn *Plessy v. Ferguson.*

After the final two justices had been persuaded to make the groundbreaking, unanimous *Brown v. Board of Education* decision in May 1954, Warren announced that "in the field of public education the doctrine of 'separate but equal' has no place. Separate educational facilities are inherently unequal." A subsequent ruling a year later ordered local school boards to desegregate schools but set no specific timetable for doing so. Unfortunately, the second decision placed federal district judges in charge of supervising the desegregation process, effectively ensuring noncompliance and opposition in the South. Still, *Brown v. Board of Education* was the landmark legal victory the NAACP had been striving for since its formation nearly a half century earlier. The decision revitalized the Fourteenth Amendment and paved the way for future civil rights legislation.

AMERICANS' REACTION TO BROWN

Many Americans—in both the North and the South—disagreed with the *Brown* decision and accused Warren of having bent the Constitution in favor of his personal opinions. On the other hand, and despite intense opposition, many Americans defended Warren's decision by arguing that he had rightly used his authority to make up for Congress's failure to protect black civil rights.

Critics of the ruling included President Eisenhower himself, who privately regretted his decision to appoint Warren to the bench. After the *Brown* decision, Eisenhower refused to support the ruling actively and therefore offered no public comment about it at all.

THE SOUTHERN MANIFESTO

Southern politicians vehemently opposed the *Brown* decision. State legislatures in Alabama, Georgia, Mississippi, and Virginia passed resolutions asserting their right to nullify federal laws they disliked. More than a hundred southern congressmen and senators even signed a "Declaration of Constitutional Principles," also known as the **Southern Manifesto**, in 1956, protesting the *Brown* decision and pressuring their home states to ignore the ruling or reject it entirely.

ROSA PARKS AND THE MONTGOMERY BUS BOYCOTT

Eisenhower's lack of support for the civil rights movement convinced many blacks that they could not rely on the federal government to right racial wrongs. Rather, many came to believe that change would have to originate within the black community itself. The first landmark change came on December 1, 1955, in Montgomery, Alabama. Black seamstress **Rosa Parks**, sitting in the "colored" section of a city bus, refused to give up her seat to a white man who was looking for a seat because the "white" section was full. Parks was subsequently arrested for disorderly conduct.

Parks's arrest outraged the black community and prompted its local leaders, including young Baptist preacher **Martin Luther King Jr.**, to organize the **Montgomery bus boycott**, refusing to ride any city buses and crippling the bus company financially. The boycott continued for more than a year, ending when the Supreme Court issued a ruling in December 1956 declaring segregated bus seating unconstitutional.

Meanwhile, King, in taking charge of the boycott, became a major figurehead in the blossoming civil rights movement. Even though he himself came from a prosperous family, he detested racial inequality and sympathized with downtrodden southern blacks. King's education, position within the Baptist church, and unmatched oratory skills made him an inspiring leader as the movement grew.

THE SOUTHERN CHRISTIAN LEADERSHIP CONFERENCE

After the success of the bus boycott, King hoped to rally more southern churches behind the civil rights cause. In 1957, King joined with nearly 100 other black ministers in founding the **Southern Christian Leadership Conference (SCLC)**. Whereas the NAACP attacked segregation via the law, King intended to use various forms of **nonviolent protest** to provoke segregationists and win support from the moderate majority of southern whites. He drew much of his inspiration from the nonviolent tactics of **Mohandas Gandhi**, who had used nonviolence to protest against British colonial rule in India. The formation of the SCLC also marked the shift within the civil rights movement from predominantly northern leadership to **southern activism**. Although the SCLC did convince more southern blacks to support the civil rights movement, the organization failed to spark controversy or elicit sympathy from whites.

THE CIVIL RIGHTS ACT OF 1957

Meanwhile, northern political leaders pushed the **Civil Rights Act of 1957** through Congress, even in the wake of the events in Montgomery and encountering extreme opposition to *Brown v. Board of Education*. Eisenhower signed the bill, but only after promising southern conservatives that the bill would have little real impact on their daily lives. Although the new bill established a **Civil Rights Commission** in an attempt to protect black voting rights, the commission made little significant difference in the lives of black southerners. Still, the Civil Rights Act of 1957 was the first major civil rights legislation passed since Reconstruction, and its passage was symbolic because it signified the growing importance of the civil rights movement at the federal level.

THE LITTLE ROCK CRISIS

Facing a tough reelection campaign in 1957, Arkansas governor **Orval Faubus** capitalized on the *Brown* controversy by defying the federal court order to desegregate public schools. Faubus positioned Arkansas National Guardsmen outside **Central High School** in Little Rock to prevent nine black students from entering. He then organized an angry white mob outside the school to protest integration and attack black reporters.

Although Eisenhower himself opposed integration, Faubus's decision to challenge federal authority forced the president to intervene on behalf of the students and end the **Little Rock crisis**. Eisenhower placed the National Guard under federal authority and sent 1,000 U.S. Army troops to disband the mob and escort the students to class. Still defiant, Faubus closed all public schools in the city for the remainder of the year to prevent "disorder."

SUMMARY & ANALYSIS

NONVIOLENT PROTEST: 1960–1963

EVENTS

1960	Greensboro sit-in occurs Student Nonviolent Coordinating Committee (SNCC) forms
1961	Freedom Rides begin Albany movement
1962	Kennedy integrates University of Mississippi
1963	Birmingham campaign turns violent March on Washington draws more than 200,000

KEY PEOPLE

Martin Luther King Jr. Baptist preacher from Georgia who became most famous civil rights leader; helped organize peaceful protests and gave keynote "I have a dream" speech at 1963 March on Washington

John F. Kennedy 35th U.S. president; gave increasing support to civil rights movement throughout his term; had plans to push stronger civil rights bill through Congress but was assassinated in 1963

Robert Kennedy Brother of John F. Kennedy and U.S. attorney general; assisted civil rights cause in the South

"Bull" Connor Birmingham, Alabama, city commissioner who ordered police violence against peaceful civil rights protesters in 1963

THE GREENSBORO SIT-IN

On Monday, February 1, 1960, four black students from the North Carolina Agricultural and Technical College in **Greensboro** sat down at the whites-only counter at a local Woolworth's and ordered lunch. The clerk refused to serve them, but the four men remained sitting at the counter until the store closed. The men returned the following day with more than a dozen fellow black students and again remained quietly at the counter until the store closed.

By the end of the week, hundreds of black students and even several white students were waiting patiently for service in Woolworth's, with several hundred more at other restaurants in Greensboro. Although the students temporarily disbanded to negotiate a settlement, the **Greensboro sit-in** resumed the following spring when local business leaders refused to cave in to the protesters' demands. Blacks continued to boycott segregationist stores such as Woolworth's until the desperate merchants finally conceded that summer.

NONVIOLENT CAMPAIGNS

The success of the Greensboro sit-in prompted thousands of blacks to launch similar campaigns in other cities throughout the South. Although police arrested thousands of protesters, most sit-ins succeeded. In 1960, for example, police arrested nearly a hundred peaceful student protesters at Atlanta University. In addition to demanding equality at city lunch counters, the students called for better jobs, better education, and social services for Atlanta's black community. Despite the arrest, other Atlanta students pledged their commitment to nonviolence, conducted sit-ins at restaurants all over the city, and organized a massive boycott of segregated businesses around Atlanta. Martin Luther King Jr. joined the students and was even among those arrested. Just as in Greensboro, hurting local businessmen eventually gave in and desegregated their stores.

THE STUDENT NONVIOLENT COORDINATING COMMITTEE

The students who participated in these sit-ins, by provoking segregationists into angry responses, succeeded in winning sympathy from whites—a tactic that Martin Luther King had wanted to employ with the SCLC. Therefore, King dispatched SCLC director **Ella Baker** to Raleigh, North Carolina, to help organize students and encourage younger blacks to join the nonviolent civil rights struggle.

With Baker's help, the students formed the **Student Nonviolent Coordinating Committee (SNCC)** in 1960. The SNCC's greatest advantage was its youthful membership—students were always willing to pack up and move to fight the next fight. The SNCC members organized hundreds of protests throughout the South in the 1960s and participated in every major campaign.

A RIFT WITHIN THE MOVEMENT

Not all civil rights activists supported the SNCC, however. Many black leaders believed the student movement was too radical and provocative. They feared that the sit-ins would destroy the small concessions that had taken them years to win from white segregationists. As a result, many all-black schools in the South punished and even expelled student protesters. The sheer success of student-led sit-ins, though, won blacks sympathy from many whites, an accomplishment that leaders such as King knew would be necessary in order to change the status quo.

THE ELECTION OF 1960

Not surprisingly, civil rights became a major issue in the 1960 presidential campaign. Although Republican candidate **Richard M. Nixon** would not admit his support publicly for fear of alienating southern conservatives, Democrat **John F. Kennedy** embraced the student-led sit-ins, mentioning them in his campaign speeches.

Kennedy's support of the movement won him the vast majority of black votes in the North, contributing significantly to his victory over Nixon that year.

KENNEDY AND CIVIL RIGHTS

Kennedy's victory was bittersweet: even though he won the presidency, Republicans and southern conservative Democrats triumphed in Congress, severely limiting Kennedy's ability to pass civil rights legislation. Nonetheless, Kennedy was able to create the **Committee on Equal Employment Opportunity** to help end racial discrimination in the federal government and strengthened the civil rights division at the Justice Department. He also ordered his brother, Attorney General **Robert F. Kennedy**, to support civil rights activism as much as he could.

FREEDOM RIDES

Kennedy's opportunity to demonstrate presidential support for the civil rights movement came the following year. In 1961, the Congress of Racial Equality organized a biracial **Freedom Ride** on interstate buses traveling through the South. CORE hoped that the Freedom Ride would provoke a reaction from segregationists just as the student-led sit-ins had, with public harassment, arrests, and widespread media attention. However, CORE also hoped that the publicity and arrests would force the Kennedys to intervene.

Black and white **Freedom Riders** left Washington, D.C., in May 1961 and faced only mild opposition until they met a mob of white supremacists ten days later in Alabama. The mob torched the bus and assaulted the Freedom Riders on board, nearly killing two of them. Another segregationist mob attacked them again in Birmingham as police looked on. Wounded and unsuccessful, the riders returned to the North and let the SNCC Freedom Riders take over. These new riders encountered severe opposition in Montgomery, Alabama, where yet another mob attacked the students. Police eventually arrested the SNCC Freedom Riders on charges of disturbing the peace.

Just as the protesters had hoped, the mob violence and police inaction in Birmingham and Montgomery outraged President Kennedy and were a major embarrassment for the U.S. government. In response, Kennedy sent 400 federal agents to prevent further violence in Montgomery and pushed the **Interstate Commerce Commission** to clarify its regulations regarding segregation on interstate buses. The success of the CORE and SNCC Freedom Rides prompted chapter organizations to sponsor their own rides in the Deep South throughout the 1960s.

THE UNIVERSITY OF MISSISSIPPI

A year after the Freedom Rides, yet another segregation crisis occurred at the University of Mississippi, prompting the president once again to act on behalf of civil rights activists. A federal court ordered the university to admit **James Meredith**, the university's first black transfer student. As Arkansas governor Orval Faubus had refused to allow black students to attend an all-white high school in 1957, Mississippi governor **Ross Barnett** and state officials refused to let Meredith enter the university.

Kennedy dispatched hundreds of U.S. marshals to protect Meredith and forcibly integrate the university. Barnett continued to resist even after the marshals arrived, organizing several thousand whites to attack them. The riot left two people dead and hundreds wounded. Kennedy then ordered 5,000 U.S. Army soldiers to secure the university and escort Meredith to class. The president also used federal troops to integrate the **University of Alabama** the following year.

THE ALBANY MOVEMENT

Hoping to continue the attention-getting campaign, SNCC and NAACP activists in the small town of Albany, Georgia, launched a massive boycott of and sit-in at local restaurants and department stores from 1961 to 1962. Martin Luther King Jr. and the SCLC eventually joined the movement to make Albany the new focus of the civil rights cause. Local police, however, refused to let the **Albany movement** turn into a national fiasco, instead protecting protesters from angry white mobs and treating the activists with civility. Even King's two arrests in Albany failed to garner national media attention, and the movement eventually collapsed. Paradoxically, Albany demonstrated the necessity for violent white reactions to civil rights protests in order to make the "love and nonviolence" philosophy work.

THE BIRMINGHAM CAMPAIGN

The failure in Albany spurred the SCLC to redouble its efforts. In 1963, King and his fellow activists organized a massive rally in **Birmingham**, Alabama, arguably the most segregated city in America. Once again, the activists organized boycotts and sit-ins to goad white residents and city officials into reacting. In an unprecedented move, King organized hundreds of Birmingham high school students to protest segregation in a **"children's crusade,"** hoping that images of persecuted youngsters would horrify moderate Americans.

This time, the tactic worked. City commissioner **"Bull" Connor** ordered police and firemen to use attack dogs and water cannons to subdue the peaceful protesters. Unexpectedly, many of Birmingham's black residents began to fight back, defending the activists by attacking police. Northerners were shocked as they watched the violence unfold on television. King himself was arrested again, and in jail he took the opportunity to write his influential **"Letter from Birmingham Jail,"** in which he explained the civil rights movement to his many critics. The letter was published and circulated throughout the country.

The violence in Birmingham prompted Robert Kennedy and the Justice Department to negotiate a settlement between the SCLC and city officials. The SCLC eventually agreed to end the boycotts and protests, but only after local merchants promised to hire more blacks and the city promised to enforce desegregation. Segregationists, however, protested the agreement and initiated a new wave of violence, forcing Kennedy to send 3,000 army troops to restore order in the city.

The events that took place in Birmingham and the resulting agreements changed the civil rights movement in two major ways. First, they mobilized the moderate majority of northern and southern whites against segregation. Second, the Birmingham campaign marked the first time poorer southern blacks began demanding equality alongside the lawyers, ministers, and students. The majority of blacks wanted immediate access to better jobs, housing, and education and wanted the country in general to be desegregated.

KENNEDY'S ENDORSEMENT

The growing public support for King and his fellow protesters convinced President Kennedy to fully endorse the movement and push for more civil rights legislation, regardless of the political fallout from southern conservatives. International embarrassment and accusations of hypocrisy from the Soviet Union also contributed to his decision to support the movement. In the summer of 1963, Kennedy appeared on national television and personally asked Congress to help safeguard blacks' rights. He argued that the United States could not effectively fight oppression abroad if so many

Americans lacked basic freedoms at home. He specifically wanted Congress to ban segregation and protect blacks' voting rights.

THE MARCH ON WASHINGTON

Later that summer, the SCLC, NAACP, SNCC, and CORE worked together to organize the largest political rally in American history to help convince Congress to pass the president's new civil rights bill. On August 28, 1963, more than 200,000 blacks and whites gathered peacefully in front of the Lincoln Memorial for the **March on Washington**. There, Martin Luther King Jr. delivered his famous **"I have a dream" speech**, which with surging, sermonic declarations outlined the visions of the civil rights movement and called for racial equality.

SUMMARY & ANALYSIS

POLITICAL ACTION: 1963–1965

EVENTS

1963	John F. Kennedy is assassinated; Lyndon B. Johnson becomes president
1964	Civil Rights Act of 1964 is passed Twenty-Fourth Amendment is ratified Freedom Summer
1965	Selma campaign Voting Rights Act

KEY PEOPLE

Martin Luther King Jr. Preacher and civil rights leader who received Nobel Peace Prize in 1964; went to Selma, Alabama, in 1965 to draw national attention to problems with black voter registration

Lyndon B. Johnson 36th U.S. president; former opponent of civil rights who became one of the movement's greatest supporters as president; helped pass Civil Rights Act of 1964 and Voting Rights Act

KENNEDY'S ASSASSINATION

On November 22, 1963, **John F. Kennedy** was assassinated as he rode in a presidential motorcade through Dallas, Texas. After Kennedy's death, many civil rights leaders feared that their dream of racial equality would die along with him. The new president, **Lyndon B. Johnson**, had never supported the movement. A conservative Democrat from Texas, he had opposed civil rights legislation while serving as the Senate majority leader.

SUPPORT FROM JOHNSON

However, in 1963, Johnson surprised black and white Americans alike by announcing that he would honor Kennedy's commitment to the civil rights cause and that he recognized the need for stronger civil rights legislation. Johnson supported civil rights not so much because he believed personally in the movement but because he wanted to establish himself as the new leader of the Democratic Party and take control of the issue before it spun out of control. As a result, Johnson pushed for an even stronger civil rights bill than Kennedy had ever intended to pass.

THE CIVIL RIGHTS ACT OF 1964

After months of wrangling, Johnson finally managed to convince enough southern conservatives in the House and Senate to support and pass the **Civil Rights Act of 1964**. The act consisted of a bundle of landmark laws that outlawed segregation and discrimination in public places, forbade racial discrimination in the workplace, created the **Equal Opportunity Commission** to enforce these new laws, and gave more power to the president to prosecute violators. Civil rights leaders hailed the passage of the act as the most important victory over racism since the civil rights bills passed by Radical Republicans during Reconstruction.

One interesting aspect of the Civil Rights Act of 1964 was that it outlawed not only racial discrimination but also discrimination on the basis of color, nationality, religion, and gender. Conservative southerners had actually had gender equality written into the document in the hope that it would kill the bill before it even got out of committee. However, conservatives lost their gamble, and the act passed with the gender provisions, boosting the growing **feminist movement** and protecting millions of working women.

THE TWENTY-FOURTH AMENDMENT

Later in 1964, Johnson and liberal Democrats were able to get the **Twenty-Fourth Amendment** to the U.S. Constitution ratified. Designed to help both poor whites and blacks in the South, the amendment outlawed federal **poll taxes** as a requirement to vote in federal elections.

FREEDOM SUMMER

Meanwhile, the SNCC and CORE, hoping to provoke southern extremists even further, organized a voter registration campaign in Mississippi. As in most southern states, less than 10 percent of the black population was registered to vote, even though blacks outnumbered whites in many districts. The SNCC recruited nearly 1,000 northern white college students to register voters and teach civics classes to black Mississippians in a campaign that it called **Freedom Summer**.

The SNCC's leaders believed that any violence against their young volunteers, since they were from the North, would spark even more outrage than usual among northern whites. Indeed, hundreds of Freedom Summer volunteers were beaten, bombed, shot at, or arrested over the course of the campaign. Several even lost their lives. In the most infamous case, FBI agents uncovered the bodies of three volunteers killed by Ku Klux Klan members near Meridian, Mississippi.

Despite the violence, the Freedom Summer campaign succeeded. Volunteers registered tens of thousands of black voters, many of them under the new **Mississippi Freedom Democratic Party (MFDP)**. More important, the continued violence attracted

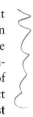

increased attention and further awakened northerners to the plight of southern blacks.

THE ELECTION OF 1964

Black leaders from the new Mississippi Freedom Democratic Party traveled to the **Democratic National Convention** in 1964 to support Johnson and promote further civil rights legislation. Democrats, however, including Johnson, refused to allow the delegates to speak and refused to recognize the party. Although Johnson still supported the civil rights movement, he feared that incorporating the MFDP into the Democratic Party would prematurely alienate conservatives and end any chance for more protective rights legislation. Although Johnson understood party politics well and his fears were justified, many MFDP activists, who thought of Johnson as an ally, were outraged. Despite the slight, blacks continued to support Johnson, who captured more than 90 percent of the black vote in the **election of 1964**. Just as important, Democrats also won control of both houses of Congress.

THE SELMA CAMPAIGN

In 1965, Martin Luther King Jr., the SCLC, and the SNCC launched yet another campaign to provoke southern whites, this time in the city of **Selma**, Alabama. The activists chose Selma because although blacks outnumbered whites in the city of nearly 30,000, only several hundred were registered voters. Tens of thousands of black protesters petitioned for the right to vote outside Selma City Hall, without success. Then, when the protesters marched peacefully from Selma toward the governor's mansion in Montgomery after a Sunday church sermon, heavily armed police attacked the protesters with tear gas and clubs, injuring and nearly killing many and arresting thousands. The violence was highly publicized, and **"Bloody Sunday,"** as the media dubbed it, shocked Americans in the North more than previous injustices.

THE VOTING RIGHTS ACT

The events in Selma also angered President Johnson, who immediately summoned Congress in a special televised session, requesting strong legislation to protect black voters. An equally angry Congress overwhelmingly passed the epochal **Voting Rights Act** in 1965. The new law banned literacy tests as a prerequisite for voting and sent thousands of federal voting officials into the South to supervise black voter registration. As a result, the black voter registration rate jumped dramatically, in some places from less than 10 percent to more than 50 percent. In effect, the Voting Rights Act finally accomplished what Radical Republicans had intended with the **Fifteenth Amendment** nearly a century earlier, in 1870. Although the Voting Rights Act did not end segregation, it began a positive transformation in the South.

BLACK POWER: 1952–1968

EVENTS

1952	Malcolm X begins speaking for the Nation of Islam
1965	Malcolm X is assassinated Watts riots break out in Los Angeles
1966	Black Panther Party forms
1968	Martin Luther King Jr. is assassinated

KEY PEOPLE

Martin Luther King Jr. Nonviolent civil rights leader; was assassinated in Memphis in 1968

Elijah Muhammad Militant black separatist leader and leader of Nation of Islam from 1934 to 1975; teachings inspired Malcolm X

Malcolm X Voice of Nation of Islam in the 1950s and early 1960s; initially preferred militant tactics as opposed to King's strategy of nonviolence but later changed his views and began working with nonviolent organizations; assassinated in 1965

Stokely Carmichael SNCC leader who expelled white members in 1966 and called for independence, self-reliance, and black nationalism in 1967 book *Black Power*

THE MILITANT MOVEMENT

Even though **Martin Luther King Jr.** had waged a successful campaign against Jim Crow laws in the South, a growing number of younger activists began to feel that nonviolent tactics could not right every social and political injustice. Blacks might have won the right to vote, eat at white lunch counters, sit at the front of the bus, and attend white colleges, but most still lived in poverty. True social change, many argued, would come only with revolution, not integration. These **militant activists** grew more and more powerful, until they came to dominate the civil rights movement in the late 1960s.

THE NATION OF ISLAM

One of the earliest pushes for **black nationalism** during the civil rights movement was the formation of the **Nation of Islam** in Detroit in 1930. Under the leadership of **Elijah Muhammad**, the organization was built upon the ideas of Marcus Garvey and the "New Negro," working to uplift impoverished blacks in the Detroit ghetto by fostering a sense of **black pride**. The Nation of Islam also operated a number of shops and restaurants to promote economic independence. Like Garvey, Muhammad stressed the importance of appreciating black cultural roots and distinctiveness. On the other hand, Muhammad saw all whites as enemies and "blue-eyed devils" and therefore rejected calls for integration. The Nation continued to spread to other cities in the East through the 1950s.

MALCOLM X

Although Elijah Muhammad was instrumental in the early development of the Nation of Islam, a young black preacher, **Malcolm X**, made it famous. Malcolm Little, the son of a civil rights worker who had been murdered by a mob of racist whites, was sentenced to prison in 1946. There, he educated himself and converted to Islam, emerging as one of the country's most vocal advocates of black nationalism and militancy in the early 1950s. He joined the Chicago headquarters of the Nation of Islam in 1952 and changed his surname to "X" to represent the identity and heritage lost by black Americans during centuries of enslavement.

Like his mentor, Muhammad, Malcolm X rejected integration and nonviolence and called on blacks to defend themselves—with violence whenever necessary—to overthrow white domination. A self-described extremist, Malcolm X was one of the most dynamic civil rights speakers of the 1950s and early 1960s.

EL-HAJJ MALIK EL-SHABAZZ

After a series of scandals rocked the Nation of Islam and its founder, Elijah Muhammad, a disillusioned Malcolm X left the organization in 1964 and went on a spiritual pilgrimage to the capital of Muslim holiness, **Mecca**, in Saudi Arabia. On the journey, Malcolm X met fellow Muslims from all over the world who challenged his attitudes toward whites and prompted him to reexamine his beliefs. He eventually returned to the United States with a new name, **el-Hajj Malik el-Shabazz**, and began working *for* integration rather than against it. He also founded the **Organization of Afro-American Unity** and supported nonviolent protest. However, in 1965, not long after his return to the United States, three Black Muslim militants gunned him down in New York City, most likely in retaliation for his defection from the Nation of Islam.

BLACK POWER

Despite his premature death, Malcolm X's emphasis on self-sufficiency and armed defense was a clarion call for others dissatisfied with "love and nonviolence." For example, the leader of the SNCC, **Stokely Carmichael**, began to incorporate black nationalism into his own philosophy in the mid-1960s and eventually convinced fellow organizers to expel white members in 1966.

The following year, Carmichael and several other disgruntled SNCC leaders broke away from the SNCC and co-authored the book ***Black Power*** to promote Malcolm X's message. Carmichael went a step further than Malcolm X and began campaigning to split the United States into separate countries—one for blacks, one for whites. The term **black power**, coined in Carmichael's book, came to be synonymous with militancy, self-reliance, independence, and nationalism within the ranks of the civil rights movement in the late 1960s and early 1970s.

BLACK PANTHERS

The militant philosophies of Malcolm X also prompted frustrated activists in Oakland, California, to form the **Black Panther Party for Self-Defense**—more commonly known as the **Black Panthers**—in 1966. Unlike the SCLC, NAACP, SNCC, or CORE, the Black Panthers demanded immediate equality for all blacks, including increased and fair employment opportunities, exemption from military service in Vietnam, health care, and educational services.

Whereas Malcolm X had merely preached revolution against white domination, the Black Panthers actually prepared for war. Clad entirely in black and armed with handguns, Black Panthers patrolled urban neighborhoods in northern and western cities, on the lookout for racist violence against blacks. The organization also operated education centers and health-care clinics in black neighborhoods to help the poorest members of these communities.

The Black Panthers' extremism and willingness to use violence, however, alienated and threatened moderate whites in the North. The federal government also perceived the Panthers as a threat and cracked down on the group between 1968 and 1969, effectively dissolving the organization.

THE WATTS RIOTS

The philosophy of black power and the shift away from nonviolent tactics also reflected a growing restlessness among urban blacks. Poverty, unemployment, and the lack of education and basic health care provoked some inner-city blacks to launch riots throughout the country between 1965 and 1970. Perhaps the most destructive of these riots were the 1965 **Watts riots** in Los Angeles. For six days, more than 50,000 outraged blacks burned and looted the neighborhood, attacking whites, Hispanics, and other minorities. It took 20,000 National Guardsmen to restore order to the district, and more than thirty people lost their lives.

KING'S ASSASSINATION

During the time of heightened black militancy, **Martin Luther King Jr.** had continued to promote racial equality in the South through non-violent means. In April 1968, however, King was shot and killed with a high-powered rifle while making a speech from a motel balcony in Memphis, Tennessee. After months of searching, police finally apprehended a young high school dropout named **James Earl Ray**, who had been seen running away from the commotion at the time of the assassination. Although Ray initially admitted to killing King, he later professed his innocence and claimed that another unnamed man had fired the shot. A congressional hearing ten years later found that it was likely others had been involved in the assassination plot, but investigators made no further arrests.

Thousands of supporters attended King's funeral in Atlanta. President Johnson, who had recently ordered the FBI to investigate King for ties with Communist organizations, did not attend. King's assassination inflamed racial tensions and led to scores of riots throughout the country. When the violence finally subsided, more than 30,000 people had been arrested.

THE END OF THE MOVEMENT

King's death in 1968 stripped the civil rights movement of its greatest leader and visionary. Ideological rifts and feuds among the NAACP, SCLC, SNCC, and CORE also led to the collapse of the movement, as did Black Panther violence and revolutionary rhetoric. As a result, the movement quickly lost momentum in 1968 and 1969 as Americans shifted their focus to the worsening **Vietnam War**.

Despite the movement's unfortunate decline, these formative years of the 1950s and 1960s gave African Americans two important things: effective government backing and legislation. Landmark Supreme Court cases, such as *Brown v. Board of Education*, along with legislative landmarks, such as the Twenty-Fourth Amendment, the Civil Rights Act of 1964, and the Voting Rights Act of 1965, finally provided the solid legal framework for protecting blacks' rights in the face of decades of discrimination.

STUDY QUESTIONS &
ESSAY TOPICS

Always use specific historical examples to support your arguments.

STUDY QUESTIONS

---

1. *How were the NAACP, the SCLC, and the SNCC different? How were they similar? Which organization had the most success in desegregating the South?*

Though the NAACP, SCLC, and SNCC were all committed to non-violence and peaceful means of protesting racial inequality, they used different strategies to desegregate the South. Despite the fact that the SCLC and SNCC received more media attention in the 1950s and 1960s, it was the NAACP's legal victories that were most successful in fundamentally overturning the South's system of Jim Crow laws.

In 1957, Martin Luther King Jr. formed the Southern Christian Leadership Conference (SCLC) to coordinate peaceful protests—akin to the Montgomery bus boycott that had taken place two years earlier—against southern Jim Crow laws. He hoped that the peaceful-protest movement would gather momentum and that he would be able to rally the support of black churches—a tactic that worked well, because of the central role that the church played in the southern black community. King found his inspiration in the nonviolent protest tactics of Mohandas Gandhi and hoped, ironically, that "passive resistance" would provoke segregationists to attack his peaceful protests, attracting media attention. He knew that the movement would need media-generated sympathy from moderate whites in order to have any lasting effect.

Whereas King organized southern black churches, the Student Nonviolent Coordinating Committee (SNCC) brought together like-minded students. Ella Baker, an SCLC director, formed the SNCC along with a group of activist students after the highly successful Greensboro sit-in in 1960. The SNCC worked diligently to mobilize black and white students in the North and South to work and protest for the civil rights cause. The SNCC organized hundreds of sit-ins, boycotts, and other peaceful protests across the country to end segregation in restaurants, stores, public transportation, and other common areas. The SNCC's tactics were highly successful and gave the movement a badly needed boost after the SCLC failed to draw enough media attention. The SNCC organized or participated in nearly every major civil rights campaign of the 1960s.

Even though the SCLC and SNCC led highly successful campaigns, the courtroom victories of the National Association for the Advancement of Colored People (NAACP) had the most lasting effect on the movement's goal to desegregate the South. Had the NAACP not won these victories, it is doubtful that the movement would ever have gained as much momentum as it did. Thurgood Marshall, a brilliant lawyer working for the NAACP, attacked the "separate but equal" doctrine that justified segregation, winning a number of significant cases, including *Missouri ex rel. Gaines v. Canada* (1938), *Morgan v. Virginia* (1946), and *Sweatt v. Painter* (1950). Marshall finally scored a direct hit on the "separate but equal" doctrine in 1954 with the U.S. Supreme Court's landmark *Brown v. Board of Education of Topeka, Kansas*, decision. Marshall won a unanimous verdict with the help of Chief Justice Earl Warren, a conservative appointee who proved more sympathetic to the civil rights movement than expected. The *Brown v. Board of Education* ruling stated that segregated public schools were inherently unequal and should be integrated as soon as possible—effectively reversing the 1896 *Plessy v. Ferguson* decision, which had made and kept "separate but equal" law. This legal victory sent a message to activists throughout the country that sweeping civil rights reform was possible and imminent, prompting both black and white activists such as King, Rosa Parks, James Meredith, and student volunteers in the SNCC to take a stand and fight for integration. Without the NAACP and the *Brown v. Board of Education* decision, the SCLC and SNCC arguably would have never even formed.

Though the SCLC, SNCC, and NAACP had the uniform goal of integrating the United States, the formation of the NAACP and its legal victories in the 1940s and 1950s were the most effective steps toward concrete desegregation of the South in the mid-twentieth century. The NAACP's victories laid the foundation for the civil rights movement and empowered blacks everywhere to organize and fight for equal social, political, and economic rights.

QUESTIONS & ESSAYS

2.   Why did the civil rights movement gain momentum in
       the 1950s and 1960s?

Although blacks had been struggling for equal rights since the end of
Reconstruction, their fight for civil rights picked up speed in the
1950s and 1960s because of the Great Migration, World War II,
and the NAACP's legal victory in *Brown v. Board of Education of
Topeka, Kansas.*

Unemployment and poverty in the South prompted as many as 2
million blacks to leave their homes in search of jobs in northern cities in the years after World War I. The Great Depression and the
invention of the mechanical cotton picker in the 1940s exacerbated
these job shortages in the South by eliminating white planters' need
for sharecroppers and field hands. Additionally, as more and more
blacks migrated north to the cities, more and more white northerners left the cities for the suburbs, thus transforming inner cities into
predominantly black neighborhoods. Nonetheless, exposure to the
much higher standard of living in northern cities also made blacks
aware of the degree of income inequality that existed between
North and South, black and white. As a result, more and more
northern blacks began clamoring for jobs, education, and social services—a cry that helped launch the modern civil rights movement as
well as the Great Society.

World War II also had a dramatic effect on black Americans, as
black civil rights leaders publicized their "Double V" campaign for
victory both abroad and at home. After civil rights leader A. Philip
Randolph threatened to organize a march on Washington, D.C., to
protest racial inequality, President Franklin D. Roosevelt signed
Executive Order 8802 to desegregate defense industries. This action
alone allowed more than 200,000 northern blacks to find jobs in
various defense industries, boosting their average income consider-
ably. President Harry S Truman later desegregated the military with
Executive Order 9981 and also created the President's Committee
on Civil Rights, one of the first government committees since
Reconstruction seriously devoted to tackling racial issues. In the
years after World War II, as the Cold War began, activists wondered
how the United States could fight for freedom abroad when so many
still lacked freedom at home. Foreign dignitaries from the USSR
asked this question too and accused the United States of hypocrisy.
Growing international pressure helped convince President John F.
Kennedy to endorse the civil rights movement fully in the early 1960s.

Despite these factors, the Supreme Court's landmark *Brown v. Board of Education of Topeka, Kansas,* decision was the most important momentum builder for the civil rights movement. In 1954, the U.S. Supreme Court, with the direct influence of the NAACP's chief counsel, Thurgood Marshall, finally overturned the "separate but equal" doctrine established by the *Plessy v. Ferguson* ruling more than a half century earlier. In declaring that segregated schools were inherently unequal, the *Brown v. Board of Education* decision opened a floodgate for more attacks on southern Jim Crow laws. Empowered by *Brown,* blacks such as Rosa Parks and James Meredith took bolder steps to end segregation.

3.   *How did Eisenhower, Kennedy, and Johnson affect the civil rights movement? Which of these presidents had the most impact and why?*

Presidents Eisenhower, Kennedy, and Johnson each entered the White House with different perspectives on the civil rights movement: Eisenhower privately opposed it, Kennedy supported it tacitly, and Johnson disagreed with it personally but wanted to assume leadership of his party and put the issue to rest. Although Eisenhower indirectly helped the civil rights movement by appointing Earl Warren to the Supreme Court and taking federal control of the Little Rock crisis, Kennedy had the most direct impact on the movement. His public support for the movement forced his successor, Johnson, to support it as well. Without Kennedy's backing, blacks might never have won the necessary government protection to fight segregation and racism in the South.

President Eisenhower appointed Chief Justice Earl Warren to the Supreme Court in the middle of the *Brown v. Board of Education* case and never foresaw the previously conservative Warren supporting a liberal cause such as civil rights. Eisenhower had never been a friend of the civil rights movement and had even opposed Truman's Executive Order 9981 to integrate the armed forces. He had deep regrets about appointing Warren and refused to comment on the landmark *Brown* decision publicly, let alone endorse the blossoming civil rights movement. Even though Eisenhower sent army troops to resolve the Little Rock crisis by forcibly integrating Central High School in 1957, he did so only to uphold federal authority, not to promote black civil rights. He later signed the Civil Rights Act

of 1957 as a political gesture, but only after assuring southern legis-
lators that the act would have no significant impact.

Whereas Eisenhower privately opposed the movement, Kennedy
privately supported it and met frequently with civil rights leaders in
the SCLC, NAACP, and CORE. Initially, he felt that he could not
endorse the movement publicly out of fear of alienating conservative Democrats in Congress. Later, however, mob violence against
the Freedom Riders in 1961 and against peaceful protesters in Birmingham, Alabama, in 1963, prompted Kennedy to back the civil
rights movement publicly, even at the risk of his own political
future. He supported the March on Washington later that year and
planned to push a new, stronger civil rights bill through Congress
but was assassinated before any such bill could be passed.

Kennedy's support for the movement effectively forced his successor, Lyndon B. Johnson, to back it as well, even though Johnson
had opposed civil rights legislation during his twelve years as Senate
majority leader. Johnson realized that he had to honor Kennedy's
commitment to the movement in order to unite the Democratic
Party and lead it effectively. He therefore put all his energy into
pushing the Civil Rights Act of 1964, a tougher civil rights bill than
even Kennedy had envisioned. Johnson later followed through with
the Voting Rights Act of 1965. Even though these acts were landmark achievements and finally gave black Americans equal social
and political rights, Johnson likely would not have endorsed them
had it not been for Kennedy's prior commitment. In fact, after
Johnson had done what he considered to be his political duty, he
ordered the FBI to investigate civil rights activists and organizations
for alleged ties to Communism.

Kennedy's public endorsement of civil rights during his final year
in office thus had a greater impact on the movement than any other
presidential actions over the movement's lifespan. Kennedy's decisions reversed eight years of opposition from Eisenhower and
forced Johnson to continue to support the movement after
Kennedy's assassination.

SUGGESTED ESSAY TOPICS

1. *How did earlier civil rights leaders, such as Booker T. Washington, W. E. B. Du Bois, and Marcus Garvey, influence the civil rights movement of the 1950s and 1960s?*

2. *Where did the term and philosophy "black power" come from? Why did black activists turn to violence in the mid- to late 1960s?*

3. *Why did the civil rights movement fall apart in the late 1960s and early 1970s? Was the movement a success?*

4. *How did Malcolm X and the Black Panthers affect the goals of the civil rights movement?*

5. *How was the civil rights movement of the 1950s and 1960s a continuation of the Reconstruction-era struggle for blacks to achieve equality?*

6. *Were the SCLC's and the SNCC's strategies of nonviolence successful?*

REVIEW & RESOURCES

QUIZ

1. Booker T. Washington and W. E. B. Du Bois disagreed on the issue of racial equality in that

   A. Washington fought for social and economic equality, whereas Du Bois fought primarily for social equality
   B. Du Bois fought for both social and economic equality, but Washington fought for only economic equality
   C. Washington strove for economic equality, whereas Du Bois fought only for social equality
   D. Du Bois fought for political equality in the South, whereas Washington fought for political equality in the North

2. Whose writings and practices inspired Martin Luther King Jr. and other nonviolent civil rights protesters?

   A. James Meredith
   B. Mohandas Gandhi
   C. Henry David Thoreau
   D. Ralph Waldo Emerson

3. Kennedy demonstrated his support for the civil rights movement most clearly when he

   A. Used federal troops to desegregate the University of Mississippi
   B. Used federal troops to desegregate public schools in Little Rock, Arkansas
   C. Signed the Voting Rights Act of 1965
   D. Attended Malcolm X's funeral

4. All of the following civil rights organizations employed nonviolent methods of protest *except*

    A. The SNCC
    B. The SCLC
    C. CORE
    D. The Black Panthers

5. Which earlier decision did the Supreme Court's 1954 *Brown v. Board of Education of Topeka, Kansas*, decision reverse?

    A. *Milliken v. Bradley*
    B. *Roe v. Wade*
    C. *Plessy v. Ferguson*
    D. *Dred Scott v. Sanford*

6. The Supreme Court ruled in *Brown v. Board of Education of Topeka, Kansas*, that

    A. Affirmative action constituted reverse discrimination
    B. Poll tax requirements for voting in federal elections were illegal
    C. Segregated public facilities were unconstitutional
    D. Companies could not use intelligence tests to screen potential employees

7. During what event did Martin Luther King Jr. first become a nationally prominent figure?

    A. The Selma campaign
    B. Freedom Summer
    C. The Watts riots
    D. The Montgomery bus boycott

8. "Revolution is bloody, revolution is hostile, revolution knows no compromise, revolution overturns and destroys everything that gets in its way. And you, sitting around here like a fly on the wall, saying, 'I'm going to love these folks no matter how much they hate me.'" The "you" in this speech probably refers to

   A. Malcolm X
   B. Martin Luther King Jr.
   C. Booker T. Washington
   D. W. E. B. Du Bois

9. "In the process of gaining our rightful place, we must not seek to satisfy our thirst for freedom by drinking from the cup of bitterness and hatred." These words were most likely spoken by

   A. Martin Luther King Jr.
   B. Stokely Carmichael
   C. Malcolm X
   D. Elijah Muhammad

10. "Whoever heard of a revolution where [protesters] lock arms . . . singing, 'We Shall Overcome'? You don't do that in a revolution. You don't do any singing—you're too busy swinging." This speech was probably made by

    A. Marcus Garvey
    B. Martin Luther King Jr.
    C. Malcolm X
    D. W. E. B. Du Bois

11. Violence against peaceful civil rights protesters in Selma, Alabama, prompted the

    A. March on Washington
    B. Passage of the Voting Rights Act
    C. Passage of the Civil Rights Act of 1957
    D. Watts riots

12. Which president supported the civil rights movement the *least*?

    A. Harry Truman
    B. Dwight Eisenhower
    C. John F. Kennedy
    D. Lyndon B. Johnson

13. What did the Voting Rights Act of 1965 do?

    A. Outlawed literacy tests
    B. Sent federal authorities to the South to help blacks register to vote
    C. Dramatically boosted blacks' political participation in the South
    D. All of the above

14. Malcolm X was initially affiliated with the

    A. Student Nonviolent Coordinating Committee
    B. Southern Christian Leadership Conference
    C. Nation of Islam
    D. National Association for the Advancement of Colored People

15. What did Executive Order 9981 do?

    A. Desegregated the military
    B. Gave blacks the right to vote
    C. Outlawed lynching
    D. Outlawed racial discrimination in factories during wartime

16. Lyndon B. Johnson threw his support behind the civil rights movement so he could

    A. Escalate the Vietnam War
    B. Unify the Democratic Party
    C. Authorize COINTELPRO
    D. None of the above

REVIEW & RESOURCES

17. During what event did Martin Luther King Jr. deliver his famous "I have a dream" speech?

    A.   The Selma campaign
    B.   The Birmingham campaign
    C.   The March on Washington
    D.   The Montgomery bus boycott

18. Blacks in Montgomery, Alabama, boycotted public transportation for a year after

    A.   Ku Klux Klansmen burned a local church
    B.   Rosa Parks was arrested for refusing to give her seat on a bus to a white man
    C.   The Supreme Court ruled that black and white children would be bused to school in separate school buses
    D.   The Supreme Court issued its *Brown v. Board of Education* ruling

19. Who was the first African American to serve on the Supreme Court?

    A.   Clarence Thomas
    B.   Earl Warren
    C.   Thurgood Marshall
    D.   James Meredith

20. In the early twentieth century, civil rights activist Marcus Garvey pushed for

    A.   Resettling all American blacks in Africa
    B.   Additional constitutional amendments to protect black rights
    C.   A race war
    D.   A national minimum wage for all workers, regardless of race

21. Jackie Robinson made headlines in 1947 when he

   A. Formed the NAACP
   B. Became the first black U.S. senator
   C. Was lynched by Ku Klux Klansmen for kissing a white woman in public
   D. Became the first black man to play for a Major League Baseball team

22. All of the following statements accurately characterize the civil rights movement between 1940 and 1970 *except*

   A. More and more activists advocated the use of violence after the mid-1960s
   B. Martin Luther King Jr. served as the movement's unofficial leader from 1955 until his assassination
   C. The first major civil rights victories for black Americans were achieved in the courtroom
   D. The failure of the sit-in tactic effectively ended the civil rights movement

23. Which methods did the NAACP primarily employ in order to achieve civil rights goals?

   A. Nonviolent methods of protest such as the sit-in tactic
   B. Violence to push for social change
   C. Legal tactics to win victories for the movement
   D. Religious tactics to encourage churches to support the movement

24. The Civil Rights Act of 1957

   A. Was a landmark law in the history of the movement
   B. Was passed after the brutal Selma campaign
   C. Was successful in increasing the number of black voters in the South
   D. Had no significant impact

REVIEW & RESOURCES

25. Eisenhower sent federal troops to desegregate public high schools in Little Rock, Arkansas, in 1957 mainly because

   A.   He personally agreed with the Supreme Court's decision in *Brown v. Board of Education of Topeka, Kansas*
   B.   Governor Faubus's use of the National Guard to prevent integration challenged federal authority
   C.   He feared riots would erupt throughout the South
   D.   All of the above

26. Which organization did Martin Luther King Jr. found?

   A.   The SCLC
   B.   The SNCC
   C.   CORE
   D.   The NAACP

27. What was President Eisenhower's response to the *Brown v. Board of Education* decision?

   A.   He fully supported it
   B.   He publicly denounced it
   C.   He tacitly supported it
   D.   He said nothing

28. The Twenty-Fourth Amendment

   A.   Prohibited segregation in all public places
   B.   Outlawed poll taxes as a requirement for voting in federal elections
   C.   Allowed blacks to vote for the first time
   D.   Lowered the voting age from twenty-one to eighteen

29. What happened during the Freedom Summer campaign of 1964?

    A. Civil rights activists boarded interstate buses in the South to protest racial segregation

    B. White activists from the North held voter registration drives in the South

    C. Over a million blacks moved to the North from the South

    D. Martin Luther King Jr. led 200,000 people in the March on Washington

30. In which city did the most infamous and destructive race riots of the mid- to late 1960s occur?

    A. Los Angeles

    B. Detroit

    C. Atlanta

    D. Baltimore

31. The SNCC was launched to organize more protests like

    A. The Montgomery bus boycott

    B. The Freedom Rides

    C. The Greensboro sit-in

    D. The Selma campaign

32. Although blacks had been struggling for equality for more than a century, the push for equality picked up momentum in the mid-twentieth century for all of the following reasons *except*

    A. More than a million blacks served in the Allied forces during World War II

    B. Millions of blacks moved to the North during the Great Depression

    C. Postwar prosperity drastically increased income inequality

    D. Eisenhower made civil rights one of his primary goals

REVIEW & RESOURCES

33. Who assassinated Malcolm X?

    A. Members of the SNCC
    B. Rivals within the Nation of Islam
    C. The Ku Klux Klan
    D. The CIA

34. What did Stokely Carmichael advocate?

    A. Black Power
    B. Nonviolent protests
    C. Affirmative action
    D. A war on poverty

35. The SNCC differed from the SCLC in that

    A. The SCLC advocated the use of violence, whereas the SNCC did not
    B. The SNCC organized students, whereas the SCLC organized churches
    C. The SCLC sought social equality, whereas the SNCC wanted social and economic equality
    D. The SCLC was a full-fledged political party, whereas the SNCC was merely a grassroots student movement

36. All of the following were true of the Black Panthers *except*

    A. They advocated Black Power and the use of violence
    B. They operated as a political party
    C. They were based in Detroit
    D. They wore black and carried guns

37. Elijah Muhammad and the Nation of Islam preached a philosophy most similar to that of

    A. Marcus Garvey
    B. Martin Luther King Jr.
    C. Booker T. Washington
    D. W. E. B. Du Bois

38. What was the main reason Lyndon B. Johnson promoted civil rights?

    A. He wanted to distract the public from the war in Vietnam
    B. He wanted to unite the Democratic Party after Kennedy's assassination
    C. He had always supported civil rights throughout his political career
    D. All of the above

39. What did the Civil Rights Act of 1964 do?

    A. Outlawed racial discrimination in most public places
    B. Sent federal election officials to the South to register more black voters
    C. Banned poll tax requirements for voting in federal elections
    D. Was more a symbolic act of Congress than a significant piece of civil rights legislation

40. The Civil Rights Act of 1964 differed from all previous pieces of civil rights legislation and Supreme Court decisions in that it

    A. Specifically protected blacks' right to vote in federal elections
    B. Banned segregation in federal offices
    C. Also outlawed gender discrimination
    D. Said that there was no scientific justification for racial discrimination

41. Most modern historians regard the civil rights movement of the mid-twentieth century as a continuation of the longer struggle for racial equality that began during

    A. Reconstruction
    B. The Great Depression
    C. The Revolutionary War
    D. The Roaring Twenties

REVIEW & RESOURCES

42. What was the de facto motto of civil rights activists in the 1950s and 1960s?

    A.   "We Shall Overcome"
    B.   "Liberty and Justice for All"
    C.   "E Pluribus Unum"
    D.   "Live and Let Live"

43. Which best describes President Kennedy's attitude toward the civil rights movement?

    A.   He fully supported it
    B.   He rejected it outright
    C.   He withdrew his support when the movement turned violent
    D.   He initially seemed not to care, then fully supported it

44. Why did Malcolm Little change his surname to "X"?

    A.   To represent his spiritual transformation after becoming a Muslim
    B.   To represent the black people's ancestry lost due to slavery
    C.   To represent all black Americans who had died at the hands of white supremacists
    D.   Because he hated his parents

45. James Meredith was the first African-American

    A.   Student to attend Central High School in Little Rock, Arkansas
    B.   Student to attend the University of Mississippi
    C.   Supreme Court justice
    D.   Secretary of state

46. What did Rosa Parks protest in 1955?

    A.   A black code
    B.   A poll tax
    C.   A Jim Crow law
    D.   A blue law

47. The "black power" movement was begun by disgruntled members of the

   A. SCLC
   B. SNCC
   C. Nation of Islam
   D. Black Panthers

48. CORE was similar to the SCLC in that both organizations

   A. Were founded by Martin Luther King Jr.
   B. Pushed for civil rights in the courts
   C. Advocated nonviolent means of protest
   D. Had no religious affiliations

49. What was the Southern Manifesto?

   A. The petition signed by dozens of southern congressmen and senators to protest the Supreme Court's decision in *Brown v. Board of Education of Topeka, Kansas*
   B. The title of Malcolm X's bold manifesto denouncing white supremacy
   C. The title of CORE's founding charter
   D. The title of a passionate speech delivered by Martin Luther King Jr. during the Selma campaign

50. Martin Luther King Jr. was

   A. An auto worker
   B. A politician
   C. A bricklayer
   D. A minister

SUGGESTIONS FOR FURTHER READING

BLOOM, ALEXANDER, ED. *Long Time Gone: Sixties America Then and Now.* New York: Oxford University Press, 2001.

CARSON, CLAYBORNE, ED. *The Eyes on the Prize Civil Rights Reader: Documents, Speeches, and Firsthand Accounts from the Black Freedom Struggle, 1954–1990.* New York: Penguin, 1991.

CHAPPELL, DAVID. *Inside Agitators: White Southerners in the Civil Rights Movement.* Baltimore: Johns Hopkins University Press, 1996.

DUDZIAK, MARY L. *Cold War Civil Rights: Race and the Image of American Democracy.* Princeton, New Jersey: Princeton University Press, 2001.

KING, MARTIN LUTHER., JR. *A Testament of Hope: The Essential Writings and Speeches of Martin Luther King Jr.* San Francisco: Harper, 1990.

———. *Why We Can't Wait.* New York: Signet Classics, 2000.

MORRIS, ALDON D. *Origins of the Civil Rights Movement: Black Communities Organizing for Change.* New York: Free Press, 1984.

PATTERSON, JAMES T. *Brown v. Board of Education: A Civil Rights Milestone and Its Troubled Legacy.* New York: Oxford University Press, 2002.

RAINES, HOWELL. *My Soul Is Rested: Movement Days in the Deep South Remembered.* New York: Penguin Books, 1983.

RHEA, JOSEPH TILDEN. *Race Pride and the American Identity.* Cambridge, Massachusetts: Harvard University Press, 2001.

WEISBROT, ROBERT. *Freedom Bound: A History of America's Civil Rights Movement.* New York: Plume Books, 1990.

X, MALCOLM, AND ALEX HALEY. *The Autobiography of Malcolm X.* New York: Ballantine Books, 1989.

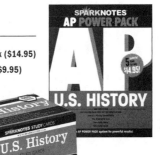